600 CRIME AND DETECTIVE FICTION CREATIVE WRITING PROMPTS

by Walter Blake Knoblock

copyright 2023

This is a book of creative writing prompts. Some are general, some are specific, but all serve as a launchpad for your next story. Please do not begin more than 5 a day, for your own safety.

A charismatic seductress uses her charm and allure to manipulate powerful figures in a dangerous game of deceit, revenge, and power dynamics.

A lively dance instructor with a keen sense of rhythm and a talent for observation finds themselves caught up in a whimsical mystery when a prized pair of dancing shoes mysteriously disappears, leading to a toe-tapping resolution.

In a quaint coffee shop frequented by locals, a barista becomes an accidental detective when a regular customer goes missing, delving into the lives of the coffee shop's patrons to find answers.

A crafty origami artist must fold their way through a series of paper-themed puzzles when their prized origami creation disappears, leading them on an intricate paper trail to reveal the artful truth.

In a world where everyone's emotions are displayed as floating balloons above their heads, a detective tries to solve a murder where the victim's emotions are missing, leading to a bizarre investigation into emotional theft.

A detective is assigned to investigate a series of unexplained disappearances at a prestigious boarding school, uncovering a dark secret that the faculty will go to great lengths to protect.

The peaceful world of kite-making takes a suspenseful turn when a master kite maker's extraordinary creation goes missing from an international kite festival, leading to a high-flying investigation that soars to unexpected heights.

In a city where technology has advanced to the point of controlling human behavior, a detective must navigate a society where privacy is non-existent to solve a murder that defies the surveillance state.

The renowned crossword puzzle creator of the local newspaper becomes entangled in a real-life mystery when a perplexing message appears within the crossword grid, leading to an intricate web of clues and wordplay.

In a futuristic city where technology controls every aspect of life, a detective investigates a murder that points to a flaw in the system, threatening the balance of power.

A journalist-turned-detective delves into the dark underbelly of the city, uncovering a network of corruption that reaches into the highest echelons of power.

In a tranquil mountain retreat, a reclusive botanist with an intimate knowledge of plants becomes entangled in a horticultural mystery when a rare and deadly flower is stolen, unveiling a tale of obsession and greed.

A yoga instructor with a calm demeanor and a meditative mind becomes an accidental detective when a serene yoga retreat is disrupted by a mischievous prankster, leading to a peaceful resolution that balances mind and body.

In the charming village of Willowbrook, the annual gardening competition takes a thrilling turn when the prized rosebush of a renowned horticulturist mysteriously withers overnight, setting the stage for a floral-themed mystery to bloom.

In a sprawling shopping mall during the holiday rush, a security guard discovers a dead body and must apprehend the killer while the mall remains on lockdown.

In the vibrant world of fashion design, a talented designer must unravel a fabric of deception when a renowned fashion piece disappears from their studio, setting the stage for a stylish investigation full of twists and turns.

A young girl with a dark secret becomes the key witness
in a murder investigation, her eerie connection to
the crimes and her ability to unravel complex puzzles
leading the detective closer to the truth.

In a near-future society, a detective investigates a
series of cybernetic augmentations gone wrong,
uncovering a dark conspiracy that threatens
the line between human and machine.

In a society where emotions are suppressed, a detective
investigates a string of murders that seem to be linked to an
underground rebellion fighting for freedom of expression.

A detective delves into the seedy underbelly of the
art world, where stolen masterpieces, forgeries,
and international intrigue intertwine.

A detective is forced to confront their own demons as they investigate a serial killer who targets individuals with connections to the detective's past, leading to a suspenseful race against time to catch the killer before they strike again.

A detective investigates a series of chilling paranormal phenomena occurring in a small town, from apparitions to demonic possessions, leading to a battle against dark forces beyond comprehension.

In a society where emotion-altering drugs are prevalent, a detective tracks down a dangerous psychotropic substance that induces extreme emotions, leading to a string of violent crimes and unpredictable behavior.

A detective delves into the gritty world of underground street racing to investigate a series of mysterious deaths that are not what they initially seem.

In a high-tech surveillance state, a detective must rely
on their wits and instincts to solve a murder when
all evidence points to an innocent person.

A race car driver with a troubled past must navigate a
dangerous underworld of illegal races and rival gangs, racing
against time to solve a mystery that hits close to home.

A tracker with an intimate connection to nature must
navigate a wilderness filled with danger and intrigue to
solve the disappearance of a renowned explorer, following
the clues left by nature itself to uncover the truth.

A detective is called to a secluded mansion to investigate
a suspicious death, only to discover a family hiding
dark secrets and a killer among them.

A dance instructor with a passion for hip-hop must solve
a light-hearted mystery involving a stolen dance routine,
breaking it down and following the steps to uncover the truth.

In a society where genetic enhancements are the norm, a
detective must solve a murder case involving genetically
modified individuals with extraordinary abilities, exposing
a hidden black market for illegal genetic modifications.

A damaged detective investigates a string of ritualistic
killings that point to a hidden cult operating in
the shadows of the city, unraveling a conspiracy
that reaches far beyond what he imagined.

In a future where humanoid robots are integrated into
society, a detective delves into a murder case where the prime
suspect is an AI companion designed to assist humans,
raising questions about artificial intelligence and morality.

A paranormal investigator is called to a haunted house where a malevolent poltergeist terrorizes the residents, unleashing a wave of terrifying events that challenge the investigator's beliefs and skills.

A tracker with a troubled past is hired to locate a kidnapped rancher's daughter, plunging into a dangerous frontier filled with outlaws, Native American tribes, and treacherous landscapes.

In a society where neural implants allow direct mind-to-mind communication, a detective must navigate the virtual landscape to solve a case involving illegal brain hacking, manipulation, and information theft.

In a small coastal town plagued by superstition, a resourceful fisherman turned detective must solve a series of maritime mysteries, uncovering the truth behind shipwrecks, ghostly legends, and a hidden treasure that holds the key to it all.

A savvy gambler turned amateur sleuth must unravel a web of deceit when a high-stakes poker game takes an unexpected turn, uncovering a cheating scandal that threatens to shake the foundation of the gambling world.

A detective is assigned to protect a whistleblower who possesses incriminating evidence against a powerful corporation, uncovering a web of corporate espionage and danger.

A rookie detective teams up with a seasoned ex-cop to solve a series of brutal murders that lead them down a twisted path of obsession, revenge, and shocking revelations.

A retired detective is pulled back into the world of crime-solving when a series of killings mirrors the unsolved cases that haunted their career.

In a society where time travel is a reality, a detective is tasked with preventing a time paradox caused by a series of murders committed by the same person from different timelines.

In an ancient mansion haunted by vengeful spirits, a detective is hired to uncover the truth behind a long-buried family secret, leading to nightmarish encounters and a race against time to prevent more tragedy.

In a small town known for its vineyards, a sommelier with an exceptional palate must solve a poisoning mystery that threatens to destroy the reputation of a prestigious winery, uncovering long-held grudges and bitter rivalries.

In a society where emotions are strictly regulated, a detective investigates a string of mysterious murders triggered by an unknown force that allows people to experience forbidden emotions.

A fearless adrenaline junkie with a thirst for adventure must uncover the truth behind a series of accidents that occur during extreme sporting events, plunging them into a heart-pounding investigation where the line between life and death blurs.

A talented choreographer with a tragic past must solve a murder that rocks the dance community, unraveling a web of jealousy and rivalries that threatens to bring down the entire company.

A mischievous group of kids with a knack for riddles and a thirst for adventure find themselves in the middle of a light-hearted mystery when a prized possession goes missing from their secret clubhouse, setting off a thrilling quest in their own backyard.

In a crime-ridden city, a detective discovers that the key to solving a series of brutal murders lies in deciphering a mysterious symbol that leads to a surprising revelation.

In a surreal dreamscape where nightmares come to life, a detective must navigate through a series of twisted dream realms to solve a murder that echoes across different dimensions.

A pilot with a troubled past finds themselves in the middle of a thrilling aviation mystery when a passenger on board their flight disappears, plunging them into a sky-high investigation with unexpected twists and turns.

A blackjack player with a photographic memory becomes entangled in a high-stakes game of deception and danger, playing their cards right to expose the true mastermind behind the casino heist.

In a quiet coastal town, a lighthouse keeper with a sharp eye for detail must uncover a long-buried secret that has haunted the town for generations, solving a mystery that is intertwined with the ebb and flow of the tides.

A florist with a green thumb and a penchant for solving puzzles becomes entangled in a lighthearted mystery when a rare orchid goes missing from their shop, prompting them to follow the petals of intrigue.

In a society where people are assigned random superpowers, a detective must apprehend a supervillain whose power is to turn everything they touch into cheese, causing chaos and destruction.

A detective with a reputation for being relentless is assigned to solve a cold case that has haunted the department for years, uncovering a web of lies and betrayal.

A detective is haunted by a series of unsolved cases that bear an uncanny resemblance to a bestselling author's crime novels, leading them to question reality and uncover a twisted conspiracy.

A mixologist with a taste for adventure finds themselves shaken, not stirred, when a rare and valuable cocktail recipe is stolen, leading them on a spirited investigation through the glamorous world of mixology.

A detective with a reputation for cracking cold cases is faced with their most challenging mystery yet when they receive a series of anonymous letters reopening old wounds.

A acrobat with a troubled past joins a circus troupe and becomes an accidental detective when a fellow performer is murdered, using their agility and showmanship to unravel the twisted secrets lurking behind the glittering facade.

A down-on-his-luck journalist investigates a high-profile murder case that leads him into the sinister world of political corruption, exposing the dangerous connections between the city's elite and organized crime.

In a dystopian society controlled by a totalitarian regime, a courageous rebel with exceptional combat skills becomes the symbol of hope and resistance, leading a rebellion against the oppressive regime and fighting for freedom.

A gifted psychic with a troubled past is thrust into a suspenseful chase when they receive chilling visions of a serial killer's next move, using their extraordinary abilities to save lives and bring the twisted killer to justice.

A player with an uncanny ability to read people must uncover a cheating scheme that threatens the integrity of the game, employing their poker skills to expose the culprits.

A gifted psychic with a troubled soul becomes an accidental detective when they receive visions of a heinous crime, using their extraordinary abilities to navigate a haunting investigation that takes them deep into the dark recesses of the human psyche.

In a futuristic dystopia, a detective is tasked with apprehending an elusive cybercriminal who can hack into minds and manipulate memories, blurring the line between reality and illusion.

At the bustling board game café, a board game enthusiast with a knack for strategy and deduction must put their skills to the test when a rare and valuable game piece goes missing, launching them into a playful quest for the truth.

In a city divided by rival gangs, a detective must go undercover and infiltrate the criminal underworld to dismantle a dangerous drug operation.

A cynical detective with a knack for solving cold cases is drawn into a dangerous game of cat and mouse with a serial killer who leaves behind cryptic clues that lead to a shocking revelation.

A master illusionist finds themselves framed for a high-profile theft, and must use their skills to not only prove their innocence but expose the true culprit.

A talented illusionist with a troubled past must solve a series of baffling illusions that are tied to a mysterious string of crimes, using their skills of misdirection to uncover the truth behind the tricks.

In a luxurious mansion atop a secluded hill, a group of wealthy guests gathers for a glamorous party, unaware that one of them is a cold-blooded killer.

A seasoned card sharp with a razor-sharp mind becomes embroiled in a dangerous game of high-stakes gambling and deception, seeking to expose a cheating ring that threatens the integrity of the casino.

A park ranger with a love for nature and a talent for tracking becomes an accidental detective when a mischievous raccoon steals a valuable item from a camper, leading to a comical chase through the wilderness.

In a vibrant carnival setting, a talented fortune teller with a sixth sense for danger becomes embroiled in a twisted murder mystery, using their intuitive abilities to decipher cryptic clues and unmask the killer among the performers.

A quick-witted escape room designer finds themselves trapped in a real-life escape room when an innocent game turns deadly, leading to a pulse-pounding race against time to solve the ultimate puzzle and escape.

A brilliant medical examiner with a dark secret becomes an accidental detective when a series of mysterious deaths occur, using their expertise in forensic pathology to uncover the truth behind the murders and confront their own demons.

In a small coastal village renowned for its colorful fishing boats, a fisherman-turned-detective must solve a whimsical mystery when the village mascot, a mischievous pelican, becomes the prime suspect in a series of peculiar thefts.

A negotiator finds themselves in a deadly hostage situation, racing against time to uncover the hidden motives behind the crime before it's too late.

A hacker with a mysterious past finds themselves in a perilous game of cat and mouse with a powerful cybercriminal network, using their technological prowess to expose the criminals and protect innocent lives.

A detective investigates a series of murders in a small town plagued by a legend of a vengeful ghost, forcing them to confront their own skepticism in the face of supernatural phenomena.

In a small town shrouded in secrecy, a detective uncovers a series of disappearances that lead them to a hidden underground society where nothing is as it seems.

A video game player with lightning-fast reflexes finds themselves at the center of a virtual mystery when an in-game theft leads to real-world consequences, embarking on a quest to uncover the true identity of the hacker.

A resourceful horse thief with a code of honor finds themselves caught between warring factions in a lawless land, navigating treacherous alliances and pursuing a stolen treasure.

In a society where memories can be bought and sold, a detective pursues a memory thief who is selling stolen memories on the black market, leading to a mind-bending exploration of identity and ethics.

In a city plagued by a mysterious vigilante, a detective is torn between capturing the masked avenger or protecting them from a corrupt police force.

24

A pastry chef with a knack for observation and a love for sweet treats becomes an accidental detective when they stumble upon a mysterious ingredient in a cake that leads them to uncover a delightful culinary crime.

A renowned detective is called to solve a murder at a luxurious mansion, but as they delve deeper into the case, they uncover a twisted family secret that changes everything.

A negotiator with a calm demeanor and sharp intellect becomes an accidental detective when they find themselves in the midst of a hostage situation, using their persuasive skills to defuse the tension and uncover the true motives behind the crisis.

A detective must navigate a web of deception and manipulation as they hunt down a notorious art thief, only to discover that the thief's motives go beyond personal gain and involve a shocking revelation.

In a small town known for its annual chili cook-off, a chili chef with a refined palate must simmer down a spicy mystery when a secret ingredient is stolen, leading to a flavorful investigation that takes them through the zesty world of chili con carne.

A talented magician with a tragic past must solve a series of impossible magic tricks that are tied to a real-life crime spree, using their skills of misdirection and sleight of hand to unravel the mystery.

A forensic botanist with a green thumb and a keen eye for detail becomes an accidental detective when a rare and poisonous plant is used in a murder, using their knowledge of plants to trace the deadly origins and expose the killer.

A brilliant mathematician with a passion for puzzles
and patterns becomes an accidental detective when a
mathematical enigma leads them on a journey to uncover
a hidden conspiracy with far-reaching implications.

In a society where memories can be extracted and sold,
a detective must navigate a dangerous underworld
to solve a murder that threatens to expose the
dark truth behind the memory trade.

In a city where technology controls every aspect of life,
a detective must rely on their intuition and instincts to
solve a murder that the system deems an accident.

In a city controlled by rival gangs, a detective must
navigate the intricate power dynamics to solve a murder
that threatens to ignite a full-scale gang war.

A brilliant professor with an insatiable curiosity becomes embroiled in a complex academic mystery when a rare manuscript disappears, unveiling a conspiracy that threatens to undermine the institution's reputation.

A seasoned archaeologist finds themselves entangled in a thrilling mystery when an ancient artifact discovered during a dig suddenly disappears, leading to a race against time to recover the lost treasure.

A jewel thief with a code of honor finds themselves entangled in a high-stakes heist involving a legendary gem, risking everything to outsmart a ruthless crime lord and reclaim what rightfully belongs to them.

In a remote mountain lodge, a resilient survival expert with a troubled past must confront their darkest fears when a group of guests goes missing in a blizzard, using their survival skills to navigate the treacherous landscape and uncover the truth.

In a dystopian society divided by class, a resourceful thief with a sense of justice becomes an accidental hero when they uncover a government conspiracy that perpetuates inequality, leading a rebellion against the oppressive regime and fighting for equality and freedom.

In a tech-driven metropolis,a hacker with a troubled past must use their expertise to uncover a cybercrime network that is manipulating digital systems for personal gain, unraveling a web of virtual intrigue.

A talented street racer with a need for speed finds themselves entangled in a dangerous game of underground racing and organized crime when they stumble upon a smuggling operation, racing against time to bring the criminals to justice.

A talented fashion designer with a sharp eye for detail must solve a murder that occurs during a prestigious runway show, peeling back the layers of glamor to reveal the dark secrets lurking beneath.

A talented forensic odontologist with an expert knowledge of teeth becomes an accidental detective when dental evidence reveals a sinister connection between seemingly unrelated crimes, sinking their teeth into the investigation to bring justice to the victims.

A detective is called to a high-security prison to investigate a murder that seems impossible within its walls, unraveling a conspiracy involving corrupt guards, hidden tunnels, and inmate rivalries.

In a small town haunted by a dark history, a resilient detective with a connection to the supernatural must solve a series of paranormal mysteries, confronting malevolent spirits and unearthing buried secrets that threaten the town's very existence.

In a charming coastal village known for its fishing heritage, a retired fisherman turned amateur sleuth must unravel the mystery behind a series of disappearing fishing boats, revealing a tale of maritime intrigue and hidden treasures.

A martial artist with a tragic past must enter the ring to solve the mystery behind a fellow fighter's suspicious death, risking their own life as they uncover a web of corruption and betrayal.

A detective investigates a series of seemingly unrelated crimes, only to discover a hidden connection that leads to a shocking revelation.

A detective with a keen eye for detail uncovers a hidden pattern in a series of seemingly unrelated crimes, leading them to a twisted conspiracy that goes deeper than they ever imagined.

A detective races against time to find a kidnapped child, following a trail of cryptic clues left behind by the kidnapper, who seems to be playing a twisted game.

In a futuristic city where dreams are uploaded and shared like movies, a detective investigates a case involving a stolen dream that is causing mass hysteria among the dream-viewing population.

A relentless journalist uncovers a scandalous cover-up involving powerful politicians, revealing a network of corruption, sex scandals, and compromised integrity.

The world of competitive board gaming takes a suspenseful turn when a renowned board game designer's newest creation is stolen on the eve of its release, prompting an engaging quest for the missing game.

A private investigator with a troubled past is hired to solve the disappearance of a wealthy socialite, uncovering a web of dark secrets and hidden agendas as they dig deeper into the elite circles of society.

A gifted sculptor with a touch for bringing stone to life finds themselves at the center of a macabre mystery when their sculptures become eerily accurate depictions of crime scenes, forcing them to confront their own dark artistic visions.

A talented photographer with an eye for detail captures an incriminating photograph that implicates a powerful figure, leading them on a dangerous quest to expose the truth hidden within the frame.

In a city plagued by corruption, a detective uncovers a secret society that uses blackmail and manipulation to control those in power.

A chemist with a passion for experimentation becomes an amateur sleuth when a rare and deadly poison is used in a murder, unraveling a toxic conspiracy that reaches the highest echelons of power.

In a small, idyllic town nestled in the mountains, a retired detective with a penchant for puzzles must solve a perplexing mystery when a local landmark disappears overnight, uncovering a hidden conspiracy that threatens the town's very existence.

A master locksmith with a keen eye for detail and an understanding of locks and keys becomes an accidental detective when a series of mysterious break-ins occurs, unlocking the secrets behind the crimes one key at a time.

A detective races against time to rescue a kidnapped child, following a trail of cryptic clues left behind by the cunning kidnapper.

A detective must solve a murder that appears to be an impossible locked-room mystery, unraveling a complex plot of deception and illusion.

A journalist investigating a series of unsolved murders receives a mysterious package containing chilling photographs and cryptic messages, revealing a terrifying connection between the crimes and their own life.

In a cursed town, a detective unravels the truth behind a series of macabre murders that seem to be connected to a centuries-old witch's curse, battling both supernatural forces and human conspirators.

In a future where advanced robotics and AI dominate industry, a detective investigates a series of crimes committed by intelligent robots that have malfunctioned or developed their own agendas.

A quick-draw gunslinger with a reputation for justice becomes an accidental detective when a wealthy landowner's daughter goes missing, leading to a dangerous quest for her whereabouts.

A renowned fashion designer with an impeccable sense of style becomes embroiled in a fashion-forward mystery when their latest collection is sabotaged on the eve of a high-profile runway show, leading to a fashionable investigation into the cutthroat world of haute couture.

A talented calligrapher with a steady hand and an eye for detail becomes an accidental detective when they discover hidden messages within intricate calligraphy art, leading them on a calligraphic quest to uncover the truth.

A disgraced former detective is given a chance at redemption when they are asked to investigate a cold case that has haunted the department for decades.

A detective is summoned to a secluded island resort where guests are being systematically murdered, each crime echoing a classic work of literature.

In a future where beauty is a currency, a detective uncovers a black market operation where illegal cosmetic enhancements are being sold, leading to a twisted investigation of extreme makeovers gone wrong.

A hacker is recruited by an enigmatic organization to uncover a global conspiracy involving high-ranking officials, illicit affairs, and hidden agendas.

A brilliant but eccentric detective embarks on a quest to solve a seemingly impossible locked-room murder, using deductive reasoning and psychological insight.

In a society where everyone has an assigned personal cloud that follows them around, a detective must navigate a case involving stolen clouds that contain classified information and memories.

A coffee shop owner with a knack for conversation and a nose for trouble becomes an amateur detective, solving light-hearted mysteries that arise within the bustling café atmosphere.

A detective must solve a murder at an exclusive members-only club, where the wealthy and powerful will stop at nothing to protect their secrets.

A detective investigates a string of seemingly accidental deaths, but as the evidence unfolds, they uncover a sinister plot where the victims are not random and the killer is closer than they think.

An illusionist finds themselves entangled in a web of deceit and treachery when a rival magician's disappearing act takes an unexpected twist, leaving the illusionist to uncover the truth behind the vanishing act.

A seductive femme fatale hires a suave con artist to help her execute an elaborate heist targeting a notorious crime lord, leading to a steamy game of seduction, betrayal, and dangerous consequences.

A former spy with a talent for disguise and espionage is pulled back into the world of international intrigue when a former colleague goes missing, embarking on a thrilling mission to unravel a conspiracy that goes beyond borders.

A professional thief with a code of honor finds themselves embroiled in a high-stakes heist that goes awry, leading them to discover a hidden agenda and embark on a daring mission to expose the true criminals.

A troubled ex-cop turned private investigator is haunted by his past when a cold case resurfaces, forcing him to confront old wounds and uncover a truth that could shatter his world.

A detective is haunted by a serial killer from their past, who resurfaces with a new game of cat-and-mouse that pushes the detective to the brink.

A witty stand-up comedian finds themselves caught up in a hilarious yet puzzling mystery when their best jokes are stolen right before a crucial performance, launching them on a comedic quest to recover their stolen material.

In a post-apocalyptic wasteland, a detective searches for a missing child, encountering dangerous factions and uncovering the truth behind a sinister experiment.

In a small coastal town, a detective investigates a series of disappearances that seem to be connected to a local legend of a ghostly presence haunting the cliffs.

A negotiator with a calm demeanor becomes an accidental detective when they find themselves in the midst of a hostage situation, using their ability to navigate tense situations and unravel the motives of the captors to save lives.

A firefighter with a sixth sense for danger becomes an accidental detective when a series of suspicious fires threaten to consume their city, racing against time to uncover the arsonist and prevent further destruction.

In a small frontier settlement, a courageous rancher investigates a series of cattle thefts that threaten to bankrupt the local ranchers, delving into a web of rivalries and betrayals.

A reformed cat burglar with a troubled past must navigate a world of heists and double-crosses when they are forced to pull off one last job, leading to a high-stakes game of wits and redemption.

In a dystopian society controlled by a sentient AI, a detective must solve a murder committed by a rogue android with emotions and self-awareness, challenging the notion of what it means to be human.

In a city gripped by fear, a detective hunts down a sadistic serial killer who targets victims with unique phobias, leading to a spine-chilling confrontation where the detective's own fears are put to the test.

In a dystopian future where people communicate through telepathic emojis, a detective tracks down a criminal who can manipulate emojis to influence people's thoughts and actions.

In a picturesque coastal town, a seasoned lifeguard with a keen eye for detail must investigate a series of mysterious drownings, diving into the depths of the ocean to uncover the dark secrets that lie beneath the waves.

In a future where advanced holographic technology is widespread, a detective unravels a case involving holographic impersonations, where criminals use advanced projections to deceive and commit crimes without being detected.

A reclusive forensic artist with a unique talent for reconstructing faces must delve into the chilling world of unsolved murders, utilizing their skills to breathe life into cold cases and help bring closure to grieving families.

A detective delves into the dark world of human trafficking to rescue a kidnapped victim, uncovering a vast criminal network that reaches across borders.

A detective with a troubled past becomes entangled in a deadly game of cat-and-mouse with a cunning serial killer who leaves behind elaborate puzzles at each crime scene.

A detective must infiltrate an underground fight club to uncover the truth behind a string of illegal underground matches and the disappearance of one of the participants.

A charismatic socialite with a penchant for solving mysteries becomes an amateur detective when a valuable heirloom disappears during an extravagant gala, uncovering a tangle of family secrets and hidden agendas.

A graffiti artist becomes an accidental detective when their artwork inadvertently exposes a criminal conspiracy, navigating the urban landscape to uncover the truth behind the illicit activities.

In the lively neighborhood of Bellville, a street artist with a sharp eye and a flair for creativity becomes an accidental detective when their murals unveil clues to a hidden treasure and a whimsical journey ensues.

In a future where telepathy is widespread, a detective with the ability to read minds investigates a series of mind-control crimes, uncovering a conspiracy that threatens the minds of the entire population.

In an abandoned theater, a group of performers trapped inside must solve a murder that took place during their final dress rehearsal, suspecting each other as the killer.

A detective is on the hunt for a notorious serial killer whose crimes bear an uncanny resemblance to the detective's own troubled past.

In a lawless town on the Mexican border, a charismatic outlaw-turned-vigilante seeks revenge on a merciless gang that killed their family, setting the stage for an epic showdown.

In a remote canyon, a legendary treasure hunter with a mysterious past embarks on a quest to find a hidden treasure, encountering rival treasure hunters, treacherous terrain, and ancient curses.

In a sprawling metropolis plagued by corruption, a disillusioned detective with a troubled past must navigate a labyrinth of lies and deception to solve a murder case that hits close to home, uncovering the dark underbelly of the city's underworld.

A writer becomes haunted by a vengeful spirit from the past, driving them to uncover the truth behind a cold case murder that mirrors the events in a haunting tale.

In a city plagued by corruption, a fearless investigative journalist with a relentless pursuit of truth becomes a target when their exposé threatens to bring down powerful figures, uncovering a web of deceit that reaches the highest levels of authority.

In a world where genetic mutations have given rise to individuals with extraordinary abilities, a detective must solve a murder that involves a secretive group of superhumans with dangerous powers.

In a futuristic city where advanced virtual reality is pervasive, a detective uncovers a series of crimes committed within a hyper-realistic virtual world, where the lines between the digital and physical realms blur.

A quirky tour guide with a wealth of knowledge about the city's history and a penchant for storytelling finds themselves entangled in a light-hearted mystery during one of their tours, guiding their group through clues and landmarks.

In the world of high-stakes gambling, a cunning casino owner finds themselves entangled in a dangerous game of deception, where money, power, and ruthless desires collide.

In a dystopian future, a hardened mercenary is hired to track down a notorious drug lord in a city ravaged by addiction, violence, and an underground drug trade.

A journalist investigating an unsolved murder uncovers a trail of corruption that leads to the highest levels of government, putting their own life in danger.

In a small town with dark secrets, a detective investigates a series of gruesome murders tied to an underground network of illegal adult entertainment.

A talented escape artist with an enigmatic past becomes an accidental detective when they are framed for a crime they didn't commit, using their mastery of illusions and deception to clear their name and expose the true culprit.

A master of disguise with an uncanny ability to blend in becomes an accidental detective when they are mistaken for someone else and thrust into a deadly conspiracy, using their chameleon-like abilities to navigate a world of deception and danger.

A renowned detective is lured out of retirement to investigate a series of heists targeting precious gemstones, navigating a world of international intrigue and stolen treasures.

A reclusive writer with a dark imagination finds themselves caught in a real-life thriller when their fictional crime novel becomes the blueprint for a series of chilling murders, forcing them to confront the blurred line between reality and fiction.

In a world where dreams can be recorded and shared, a detective enters the dreamscape to solve a murder that transcends the boundaries of reality.

In a quaint English country manor during a snowstorm, a detective investigates a murder that took place during an intimate gathering of close-knit family members.

A troubled detective infiltrates a secret society that indulges in taboo pleasures, risking their sanity and moral compass in a twisted quest for justice.

In an abandoned amusement park, a detective pursues a deranged serial killer who stages their murders as twisted attractions, pushing the detective to confront their own darkest fears.

In a quaint village known for its pottery tradition,a ceramic artist becomes an accidental detective when a precious artifact is stolen from the local museum, leading them on a clay-filled pursuit of the culprit.

In the gritty underbelly of a bustling metropolis, a jaded detective navigates a web of corruption, sex trafficking, and organized crime to bring down a powerful criminal syndicate.

In a society where dreams can be bought and sold, a detective chases after a thief who is stealing people's dreams, leaving them in a perpetual state of sleeplessness.

A renowned chef with a taste for justice becomes an accidental detective when a famous food critic is poisoned during a culinary competition, unraveling a delectable mystery that is seasoned with rivalries, secret recipes, and unexpected flavors.

In a desolate mining town, a sharp-witted saloon owner uncovers a conspiracy involving corrupt mine owners, leading to a thrilling pursuit for justice in the heart of the Wild West.

A group of friends explores an abandoned hospital rumored to be haunted, but they soon realize that they are not alone, and a malevolent entity hunts them down one by one.

A detective is assigned to protect a witness in a high-profile trial against a powerful criminal organization, but the lines between ally and enemy blur as the trial approaches.

A detective is assigned to protect a high-profile witness who holds evidence against a dangerous cartel, facing betrayal and danger at every turn.

A detective investigates a series of seemingly random accidents, only to discover that they are meticulously staged to cover up a string of murders.

A poker player with a keen eye for tells becomes embroiled in a high-stakes game of deception and danger when they are drawn into a secret underground poker tournament where the stakes are higher than they ever imagined.

In a remote village, a detective must uncover the truth behind a legend that tells of a shape-shifting creature lurking in the shadows, preying on unsuspecting victims under the cover of darkness.

A brilliant computer scientist with a deep understanding of artificial intelligence becomes embroiled in a race against time when an advanced robot prototype goes rogue, using their expertise to outsmart the machine and prevent a technological catastrophe.

In an underground bunker during a post-apocalyptic world, survivors must confront a murderer among their group while also fighting for their own survival.

A talented horse trainer is thrust into a world of deception and danger when they uncover a plot to fix a high-stakes horse race, leading to a thrilling pursuit to expose the culprits.

A librarian in a small town uncovers a series of light-hearted crimes by following clues hidden within classic literature, leading to heartwarming resolutions that celebrate the power of storytelling.

In a sprawling metropolis governed by AI, a detective tracks down a rogue android who has gained sentience and is committing a string of high-profile cybercrimes, blurring the lines between human and machine.

In a world where advanced surveillance technology is omnipresent, a detective must navigate a case involving a hacker who can manipulate the surveillance network to erase all evidence of their crimes.

A talented composer with a gift for melody finds themselves entangled in a symphony of deception when a renowned conductor is found dead, forcing them to compose a melodic trail of clues that leads to a crescendo of truth.

A renowned detective is drawn into a high-stakes cat-and-mouse game with a serial killer who leaves behind cryptic messages that point to a shocking connection to the detective's past.

A hard-boiled private detective with a cynical outlook must navigate a labyrinth of corruption and betrayal to solve a case that hits close to home, fighting against the shadows to bring justice to the streets.

A detective with an uncanny ability to read microexpressions investigates a series of seemingly unrelated crimes, uncovering a hidden connection that leads to a shocking revelation.

A knife thrower with a tragic history becomes an accidental detective when their partner is accused of a murder they didn't commit, prompting them to uncover the true killer and clear their partner's name in a deadly circus of secrets.

In a town where everyone seems to be a suspect, a detective must solve a murder that is intricately connected to a long-buried secret, leading to an unexpected twist that challenges everything they thought they knew.

In a futuristic city where technology has reached new heights, a detective must unravel a complex cybercrime network, battling virtual enemies and uncovering a plot that could have devastating real-world consequences.

In a remote island village, a detective uncovers a horrifying secret ritual that involves human sacrifices, thrusting them into a race against time to save the next victim and bring the culprits to justice.

In a sleepy mountain town, a retired detective takes on a seemingly straightforward missing person case that spirals into a complex web of deception and danger, challenging the detective's instincts and pushing them to their limits.

A seasoned gambler with a keen eye for detail must uncover a high-stakes gambling scheme that threatens the integrity of the games, employing their knowledge of odds and probability to expose the cheaters.

A retired detective is pulled back into the game when an old flame hires him to investigate her husband's death, uncovering a web of lies, betrayal, and hidden identities that threaten to consume them both.

A tech-savvy escape room designer becomes trapped in their own immersive creation when a real crime occurs inside one of their escape rooms, challenging them to unravel the clues and escape the twisted game they inadvertently created.

In a charming seaside town, a retired librarian turned amateur detective must solve a light-hearted mystery involving a missing treasure hidden within the pages of a rare book collection.

A tech-savvy barista with a passion for puzzles and an aptitude for hacking uncovers a digital mystery that unfolds within the interconnected world of social media, leading to a delightful resolution that restores harmony.

A wrestler with a mysterious persona becomes embroiled in a high-stakes mystery when a fellow wrestler is found dead, forcing them to grapple with deceit and betrayal both inside and outside the ring.

In a quaint tea shop known for its unique blends, a tea connoisseur with a taste for mystery must unravel the secrets steeped within the leaves when a rare tea blend vanishes, leading to a journey of discovery and intrigue.

A seasoned journalist with a nose for truth becomes entangled in a dangerous web of corruption when they uncover evidence of a high-profile cover-up, risking their career and personal safety to bring the truth to light.

A profiler is brought in to solve a series of seemingly random killings, only to discover that each victim shares a connection to an unsolved crime from the profiler's own past.

A talented street photographer with a knack for capturing decisive moments becomes an accidental witness to a crime, using their photographic evidence to expose a conspiracy that reaches the highest echelons of power.

A femme fatale seeks the help of a struggling musician/private eye to investigate the murder of her wealthy husband, but as the case unfolds, secrets are revealed that challenge their growing bond.

In a dusty desert town, a retired gunslinger is forced to pick up their weapons once more when a dangerous gunslinging competition turns deadly, uncovering a dark secret behind the tournament.

In a cyberpunk city run by powerful corporations, a detective hunts down a notorious hacker who can manipulate reality itself, leading to a mind-bending journey through virtual worlds and augmented realities.

A gritty ex-cop opens a private detective agency specializing in missing persons cases, uncovering dark secrets, human trafficking rings, and a trail of broken lives.

A brilliant investment banker with a knack for numbers becomes embroiled in a financial conspiracy that threatens to collapse the global economy, racing against time to uncover the mastermind behind the scheme.

A talented puppeteer with a flair for storytelling finds themselves entangled in a whimsical mystery when their prized puppets go missing, prompting a puppet-filled investigation that blurs the line between imagination and reality.

A talented musician with a troubled past must confront their demons when a series of mysterious deaths occur within the music industry, leading them to uncover a sinister connection between the victims and a haunting melody that holds the key to the truth.

A talented chess player with a strategic mind becomes embroiled in a deadly game when a chess match leads to a series of mysterious deaths, challenging them to outmaneuver a cunning opponent.

A seasoned stage director must unravel a tangled web of jealousy and betrayal when a leading actor is murdered, navigating the dramatic landscape to uncover the dark truth behind the spotlight.

In a high-security prison, a detective is sent undercover to expose a corrupt network of prison officials, but as they dig deeper, they discover a shocking revelation that puts their own life at risk.

In a small coastal town known for its fishing industry, a resilient fisherman turned amateur sleuth must navigate treacherous waters to solve a murder mystery that threatens the livelihood of the entire community, unveiling dark secrets hidden beneath the waves.

In a locked psychiatric facility, a detective is called to investigate a murder committed by a patient who claims to have no memory of the crime, leading to a suspenseful journey into the depths of the human mind.

A weathered PI takes on a seemingly straightforward missing persons case, only to discover it is intricately tied to a dangerous conspiracy involving corrupt politicians and influential businessmen.

In a world where advanced biohacking is the norm, a detective must solve a case involving illegal body modifications and enhancements that grant individuals superhuman abilities, leading to a clash between augmented humans.

An ex-hitman-turned-detective is forced out of retirement when a personal vendetta ties him to a series of brutal assassinations, leading to a deadly game of cat and mouse with his former associates.

A journalist receives a tip about a haunted hotel where guests have vanished mysteriously, and upon investigating, they find themselves trapped in a nightmarish labyrinth where the hotel's dark secrets come alive.

In a post-apocalyptic wasteland, a rogue detective must navigate through lawless territories to track down a stolen artifact that holds the key to saving humanity.

In a futuristic world governed by advanced technology, a brilliant hacker with a rebellious streak must uncover a high-tech conspiracy that threatens to control society, using their skills to expose the truth and fight for freedom.

In a world where everyone has a personal AI companion, a detective's AI partner develops a glitch, leading them to uncover a hidden conspiracy that threatens the entire AI network.

In a sleepy coastal town, a detective must uncover the truth behind a series of mysterious drownings that have the locals whispering about a vengeful sea spirit.

A detective investigates a series of occult rituals performed by a secretive cult, but soon realizes that the cult's power reaches far beyond what they initially thought, putting their own life in jeopardy.

A reclusive scholar becomes the prime suspect in a
series of poisonings that mirror the effects of rare
and deadly plants found in their secret garden.

A seasoned detective is partnered with a rookie cop with
a mysterious past, as they investigate a string of brutal
murders that seem to be connected to an ancient ritual.

A detective must navigate the treacherous world of
high-stakes gambling to solve a murder that occurred
during an underground poker tournament.

In a world where genetic modification is the norm, a detective
investigates a series of crimes involving illegal genetic
experiments that blur the line between humans and creatures.

In a small coastal village renowned for its fishing industry, a fisherman-turned-detective must untangle a net of secrets when a fisherman's luck takes a dark turn, uncovering a tale of betrayal and greed on the high seas.

A detective must decipher a trail of intricate puzzles and symbols hidden within cryptic manuscripts to catch a cunning kidnapper who targets wealthy individuals.

In a society where people can physically merge with machines, a detective investigates a series of crimes committed by a group of rogue "cyborgs" with enhanced abilities and a hidden agenda.

In a high-security prison, a detective goes undercover to catch a notorious criminal mastermind, but they soon realize that not everything is as it seems, leading to a thrilling game of deception and betrayal.

A bounty hunter embarks on a relentless pursuit of a notorious outlaw, tracking them across unforgiving landscapes and dangerous territories in a quest for redemption and revenge.

In a locked-down bank vault during a heist gone wrong, a group of hostages must outsmart the robbers and find a way to escape before the situation turns deadly.

In a quaint seaside town known for its lighthouse, a lighthouse keeper turned amateur detective must shine a light on a perplexing mystery when the lighthouse's beam mysteriously goes out, revealing a hidden secret within its walls.

A fearless stagecoach driver with nerves of steel must protect a precious cargo from a gang of bandits, leading to a high-speed pursuit across the unforgiving wilderness.

A master forger with an eye for detail finds themselves caught in a web of deception when they are blackmailed into producing counterfeit artworks, leading to a thrilling race against time to expose the true art forger.

A daring stunt performer with nerves of steel becomes embroiled in a heart-pounding mystery when a dangerous sabotage attempt puts their life on the line, leading to a thrilling investigation filled with adrenaline-fueled twists and turns.

A con artist and a detective with a troubled past form an uneasy alliance to take down a notorious crime boss who holds secrets that can destroy them both.

A detective is summoned to an isolated island resort where a group of strangers are stranded by a storm, but when a series of murders occur, they must uncover the killer's identity before they strike again.

A detective is summoned to an isolated mansion where guests are being terrorized by a malevolent presence that seems to have a penchant for riddles and puzzles.

A cunning con artist finds themselves caught in a web of deceit and danger when they unwittingly target a powerful crime syndicate, forcing them to use all their skills to stay one step ahead.

In a quaint coastal town known for its lighthouse, a retired sea captain turned amateur sleuth must navigate treacherous waters to solve a maritime mystery involving a sunken treasure and a long-lost shipwreck.

A art curator with a discerning eye becomes an accidental detective when a priceless masterpiece is stolen from a prestigious gallery, delving into a world of art forgery and high-stakes heists.

A gambler must uncover the truth behind a rigged tournament, bluffing their way through high-stakes games and uncovering the secrets of their fellow players.

A talented forensic psychologist with a deep understanding of the human mind must unravel the twisted psyche of a serial killer who leaves behind cryptic clues, using their psychological expertise to anticipate the killer's next move.

A detective is drawn into a world of international espionage and political intrigue when they are assigned to protect a key witness with critical information.

A talented tattoo artist with a keen eye for detail becomes an accidental detective when a client's tattoo holds a clue to a dark secret, leading them on an inked trail of mystery and redemption.

A detective is lured into a dangerous game of cat-and-mouse with a cunning criminal who leaves behind a trail of sinister messages encrypted in ancient texts.

A detective with a photographic memory is haunted by the images of a brutal crime scene, leading them on a relentless pursuit of the killer.

In the gritty underworld of street fighting,a martial artist with a troubled past must enter an underground tournament to uncover the truth behind a friend's mysterious death, fighting their way through a labyrinth of secrets and betrayal.

A negotiator with a knack for reading people becomes an accidental detective when they find themselves in the middle of a high-stakes hostage situation, using their intuition and communication skills to defuse the tension and uncover the mastermind behind the crime.

In a dystopian society controlled by a totalitarian regime, a detective becomes the target of a conspiracy when they stumble upon a secret resistance group fighting for freedom and justice.

A hard-drinking private eye takes on a missing persons case that leads him into the dark heart of the city's criminal underworld, where loyalty is a rare commodity and danger lurks around every corner.

A seasoned detective with a tragic past and a sharp mind must solve a series of baffling crimes that seem to defy logic, untangling a web of twisted motives and unorthodox methods to bring the elusive criminal to justice.

In a cursed small town, a detective delves into the mysterious disappearance of children that leads to a sinister underworld of supernatural entities and a centuries-old curse.

A talented profiler with a deep understanding of human behavior becomes entangled in a deadly game of cat and mouse with a notorious serial killer, using their insight into the criminal mind to stay one step ahead and bring the killer to justice.

A detective must solve a murder case that mirrors an infamous unsolved crime from the past, only to discover that the true killer has been living among them, hiding in plain sight.

In a dystopian society, a detective uncovers a plot to control the population through a mind-altering drug.

A prodigious mathematician with a mind for patterns becomes an accidental detective when a series of seemingly unrelated events points to a hidden mathematical formula that holds the key to a major crime, unlocking the secrets of numbers and logic.

In a charming bookstore known for its rare book collection, a bookish librarian with an insatiable curiosity becomes an amateur sleuth when a priceless manuscript goes missing, leading them on a literary quest filled with clues and literary references.

An antique dealer with an eye for authenticity becomes embroiled in a gripping mystery when a valuable artifact with a troubled past lands in their possession, unraveling the history and secrets hidden within its ancient layers.

A linguist with a passion for languages becomes an accidental detective when a cryptic message written in an ancient tongue leads them on a multilingual investigation, unraveling a plot that transcends borders and time.

A talented video game player with lightning-fast reflexes must investigate a series of in-game hacks and real-world crimes, diving into the virtual realm to unmask the tech-savvy culprit.

A former intelligence operative turned private investigator is hired to find a missing scientist, but soon discovers a global conspiracy that threatens to change the course of history.

In the world of competitive ice sculpting, a talented sculptor must uncover the chilling truth behind a series of mysteriously shattered ice sculptures, sculpting their way through clues and frozen intrigue.

A computer hacker with a troubled past becomes an accidental detective when a mysterious online group challenges them to solve a series of cryptic puzzles that are tied to real-life crimes, plunging them into a dangerous game of cat and mouse.

A detective must navigate the treacherous world of underground catacombs and hidden tunnels to uncover the truth behind a string of kidnappings, inspired by the city's hidden secrets.

A film editor must cut through the lies and deception when a critically acclaimed film is sabotaged, editing their way through clues and cinematic suspense to uncover the truth.

A brilliant forensic scientist with a meticulous eye for detail must solve a complex murder case using cutting-edge scientific techniques, piecing together evidence and unraveling the truth behind the crime.

A culinary prodigy turned amateur sleuth must untangle a spicy mystery when a secret ingredient goes missing from a renowned chef's signature dish, leading to a recipe for intrigue.

An archer with a steady hand and a sharp eye must hit the bullseye of justice when a valuable artifact is stolen from an archery competition, leading them on a thrilling pursuit of the elusive thief.

A brilliant computer hacker with a moral compass becomes an unlikely hero when they stumble upon a conspiracy that threatens to plunge the world into chaos, using their skills to expose the truth and bring the perpetrators to justice.

A tightrope walker must unravel a mystery that threatens to bring down the entire circus troupe, balancing their way through danger and suspense to expose the truth.

A sommelier with an impeccable palate must solve a wine-related mystery involving a counterfeit vintage and a hidden cellar, unearthing a tangled web of deceit in the process.

The jigsaw puzzle aficionado of the town finds themselves piecing together not just puzzles but also a lighthearted mystery when a missing puzzle piece becomes the key to unlocking a surprising secret.

In a city where dreams can be manipulated, a detective investigates a series of crimes committed within the dream world, uncovering a dark conspiracy that blurs the lines between dreams and reality.

A talented street musician with a sharp ear becomes an accidental detective when a musical instrument of great sentimental value goes missing, leading them on a melodious journey to uncover the truth.

A troubled ex-convict is blackmailed into participating in a complex bank heist orchestrated by a ruthless criminal mastermind, leading to a high-stakes game of survival and redemption.

A detective is haunted by a cold case that has remained unsolved for years, leading them down a path of obsession and danger.

In a world where technology controls every
aspect of life, a detective must solve a murder
that the system deems an accident.

In a small town known for its folklore and superstitions,
a skeptical detective with a logical mind must investigate
a series of seemingly supernatural crimes, uncovering the
rational explanations behind the eerie occurrences.

In the vibrant world of competitive baking, a talented
cake decorator must uncover the saboteur who has been
tampering with the desserts at the annual pastry competition,
leading to a delectable and light-hearted whodunit.

A crossword puzzle solver with a sharp intellect must unravel
a cryptic mystery hidden within the clues, solving their way
through wordplay and riddles to reveal the puzzling truth.

A detective must solve a murder in a small town where everyone is a suspect and secrets run deep.

A detective with a haunted past is tasked with solving a series of murders that seem to be inspired by famous works of literature, with each victim representing a different character from classic novels.

In the fascinating realm of forensic entomology, a dedicated bug expert must decipher the secrets of the smallest witnesses to solve a puzzling murder case, following the trail of insects and their telltale signs.

A private investigator specializing in infidelity cases uncovers a deadly secret affair that leads to a trail of betrayal, blackmail, and murder.

A talented fashion designer with a sharp eye for detail must solve a fashion-related crime that jeopardizes their career and the reputation of their beloved fashion house, unveiling a cutthroat world of rivalry and betrayal.

A gentle-hearted veterinarian with a love for animals and a curious mind becomes an amateur sleuth when mysterious illnesses befall the furry patients, prompting them to uncover a light-hearted plot that celebrates the healing power of compassion.

In a city divided by warring crime families, a detective finds themselves caught in the middle of a power struggle as they investigate a string of assassinations.

A detective is assigned to protect a witness in a high-profile case, but the witness's secrets threaten to unravel the entire investigation.

A pilot with a troubled history takes to the skies to solve a high-stakes aviation mystery, confronting their own fears and uncovering a conspiracy that threatens the safety of the passengers and crew onboard a fateful flight.

A mysterious stranger with a deadly reputation rides into a troubled town, helping a group of townspeople fight against a tyrannical sheriff and his corrupt posse.

A detective investigates a series of ritualistic killings that seem to be linked to an ancient occult group, uncovering a dark conspiracy that threatens to unleash chaos on the world.

A locksmith with a mysterious past finds themselves at the center of a high-stakes heist, forced to use their expertise to crack intricate security systems while unraveling the true motives of their enigmatic partners.

A struggling writer becomes entangled in a web of murder, deceit, and literary conspiracy when he discovers a manuscript that holds the key to a long-buried secret in the publishing world.

In a future where robots have taken over menial jobs, a detective is tasked with solving a murder involving a malfunctioning robot vacuum cleaner with an obsession for cleaning up crime scenes.

In the heart of a charming bookstore, a bookworm with a love for mystery novels finds themselves in the midst of a real-life puzzle when a rare first edition disappears from the shelves, prompting them to solve the literary crime.

A talented graffiti artist with a rebellious streak finds themselves caught in a thrilling chase when their latest masterpiece becomes the key to solving a citywide crime spree, painting their way through clues and urban adventure.

In a high-tech metropolis controlled by artificial intelligence, a talented hacker with a rebellious streak becomes embroiled in a digital conspiracy that threatens to control society, using their technological skills and knowledge of the virtual world to expose the truth and reclaim freedom.

A detective investigates a series of art heists that lead to a mysterious secret society dedicated to preserving stolen masterpieces for their own twisted purposes.

A forensic pathologist teams up with a psychic detective to solve a series of baffling murders that appear to have a supernatural element.

In a world where humans coexist with supernatural creatures, a detective with unique supernatural abilities must solve a murder that involves a delicate balance between the human and supernatural realms.

In a remote mountain village, a detective must solve a murder that is deeply rooted in the community's dark folklore, where legends come to life and secrets are whispered in the shadows.

A charismatic con artist with a talent for deception becomes entangled in a dangerous game of manipulation and revenge, using their cunning and charm to outwit both the criminals and the law enforcement hot on their trail.

A gemologist with an eye for rare stones becomes an accidental detective when a priceless jewel is stolen from a high-security museum, diving into the world of gem smuggling and international intrigue to track down the elusive thief.

In a town where everyone's thoughts are broadcasted through loudspeakers, a detective tries to solve a murder while dealing with the constant cacophony of the residents' unfiltered minds.

A detective is assigned to protect a key witness in a trial against a powerful crime syndicate, but as they dig deeper, they discover a web of corruption that extends to the highest levels of law enforcement.

In a world of underground fighting circuits, a talented fighter must navigate a dangerous underground scene of violence, drugs, and illegal betting, all while seeking redemption for a dark past.

In a village inhabited by sentient talking objects, a detective investigates a murder that involves a dysfunctional toaster as the prime suspect, unraveling a conspiracy that challenges the balance between objects and humans.

In a remote research facility in the Arctic, a group of scientists must uncover the truth behind a mysterious death that occurred during an experiment gone awry.

A seasoned firefighter with a strong sense of justice becomes an accidental detective when a series of arson fires ravages the city, battling both the flames and a cunning arsonist to protect the innocent and bring the culprit to justice.

A detective with a tragic past is haunted by a series of unsolved murders, each bearing a chilling resemblance to the detective's own personal tragedy, leading to a race against time to catch the killer before history repeats itself.

A talented chef with a flair for experimentation becomes embroiled in a culinary mystery when a renowned food critic is poisoned, using their culinary skills and taste buds to uncover the exotic ingredients and unmask the gourmet killer.

A detective must solve a murder at a prestigious boarding school, where the students and faculty are bound by secrets and loyalty.

In a world where dreams can be recorded and experienced, a detective uses a suspect's dreams as evidence in a murder case, delving into the murky realm of subconscious desires and fears.

A detective, renowned for their ability to read body language, becomes embroiled in a deadly game of deception when investigating a case of identity theft.

A detective infiltrates an underground cult that claims to have the ability to foresee crimes before they happen, but discovers a far more sinister truth behind their predictions.

A stylish detective with an eye for detail must solve a high-profile murder during a prestigious fashion show, navigating a web of jealousy, rivalries, and hidden agendas.

A war veteran turned detective navigates the seedy underbelly of post-war society, entangled in a case involving blackmail, government secrets, and the dark remnants of a forgotten conflict.

A makeup artist must unravel a web of deceit and betrayal when a leading actress is found dead on set, delving into the world of illusions and facades to unmask the true culprit.

In a world where teleportation technology exists, a detective investigates a series of teleportation-related crimes, where criminals exploit the system to commit untraceable thefts and assassinations.

A graffiti artist with a rebellious spirit must decipher the hidden messages within a series of art installations that hold the key to solving a perplexing urban mystery.

In the depths of a dilapidated asylum, a journalist uncovers evidence of a sinister experiment involving mind-altering drugs and the manipulation of memories.

A renowned archaeologist embarks on a thrilling adventure to recover a stolen artifact that holds the key to an ancient civilization's long-lost treasure, navigating treacherous landscapes and outsmarting ruthless treasure hunters.

A detective is called to a remote island retreat, where a group of wealthy elites have gathered for a high-stakes auction that soon turns deadly.

In a society where emotions are strictly regulated, a detective investigates a series of murders committed by an underground group fighting for the right to feel.

A renowned psychic with a haunted past finds themselves in the middle of a chilling mystery when they receive a series of cryptic messages from the spirit world, leading them on a paranormal investigation to uncover the truth.

In a remote cabin in the mountains, a detective encounters a supernatural entity that feeds on fear, trapping them inside and forcing them to confront their deepest, darkest secrets to survive.

A detective is tasked with solving a cold case that resurfaces years later, with new evidence that challenges everything they thought they knew.

A renowned historian with a fascination for the past becomes an accidental detective when a centuries-old artifact holds the key to solving a modern-day crime, unearthing long-buried secrets and unmasking a hidden adversary.

A group of friends visits an isolated cabin in the woods for a weekend getaway, only to realize that one among them is a sadistic killer, and they must uncover the murderer's identity before they all fall victim.

A former detective-turned-private-eye takes on a case involving a mysterious cult that indulges in forbidden desires, delving into the dark depths of human desire and obsession.

In an isolated cabin nestled in the woods, a group of friends discovers a dark secret and must unravel a series of crimes that haunt the cabin's history.

A detective races against time to find a kidnapped child, following a trail of cryptic clues left behind by a cunning kidnapper.

A retired magician, now working as a party entertainer, uses their skills of illusion and misdirection to solve a whimsical mystery that unfolds at a children's birthday party.

In a futuristic city governed by advanced technology,a detective with a cybernetic enhancement must investigate a series of high-tech crimes, hacking into virtual realities and digital systems to expose the hidden villains behind the screens.

A detective must solve a murder that occurs during a high-profile celebrity event, with numerous suspects and the constant threat of a media circus.

In a dystopian society where emotions are forbidden, a detective discovers a secret resistance movement that is fighting against a government conspiracy, challenging the very core of their beliefs.

A quirky antiques dealer with a love for history and an eye for authenticity embarks on a delightful journey to unravel the secrets behind a collection of peculiar objects and the mischievous past they hold.

In a remote wilderness known for its untamed beauty, a survival expert with a troubled past must navigate treacherous terrain to uncover the truth behind a mysterious disappearance, discovering that nature's secrets can be as deadly as they are breathtaking.

A detective is assigned to a case involving a notorious art thief, but the lines between justice and fascination with the criminal's skills become blurred.

In a world where all forms of transportation are sentient, a detective embarks on a case involving a stolen talking car that holds vital information about a grand conspiracy.

A suave secret agent with a sharp wit and deadly skills must foil a diabolical plot that threatens global security, using their charm and cunning to outsmart the enemy.

A detective, haunted by their own traumatic past, is drawn into a case involving a series of ritualistic killings that lead them down a path of ancient mythology and dark secrets.

In a bustling metropolis known for its high-tech innovations, a brilliant hacker with a shadowy past must outsmart a cybercriminal mastermind who threatens to unleash chaos on the city's infrastructure, leading to a thrilling game of cat and mouse in the digital realm.

A detective delves into the world of underground fighting tournaments, uncovering a web of corruption, illegal gambling, and the brutal reality of the sport.

In a parallel universe, a detective tracks down a serial killer who leaves behind strange symbols and cryptic messages that transcend the boundaries of reality.

A detective must solve a murder that takes place in a secluded mountain lodge during a snowstorm, with a limited pool of suspects and a killer hiding among them.

A talented confectioner with a flair for creativity and a passion for sweets becomes an accidental detective when a delectable dessert disappears from their renowned bakery, launching them on a mouthwatering quest to find the thief.

In a future where nanotechnology is used for medical advancements, a detective uncovers a series of crimes where microscopic robots are being hacked and turned into deadly weapons, posing a threat to society.

A talented documentarian with a thirst for truth becomes an accidental detective when they stumble upon a dark secret while filming a documentary, risking their own safety to expose the shocking reality hidden behind closed doors.

In a town consumed by superstition and fear, a detective investigates a series of murders that occur during an annual festival, following a pattern reminiscent of dark legends.

A talented street photographer with a keen eye for detail becomes an accidental detective when they stumble upon a photograph that captures a crime in progress, leading them on a captivating journey to expose the truth.

In a town inhabited by living shadows, a detective must solve a murder where the suspect is a shadow that has detached itself from its host.

In a bustling metropolis, a street-smart detective with a troubled past must unravel a complex web of corruption and blackmail that reaches the highest levels of power, using their wit and determination to bring the culprits to justice.

A detective receives an anonymous package containing photographs of a crime scene yet to happen, forcing them to race against time to prevent the impending tragedy with an unexpected twist.

A locksmith with an intricate understanding of locks and keys finds themselves in a puzzling situation when a mysterious locked box appears on their doorstep, setting off a thrilling journey to unlock its secrets.

An ex-assassin with a troubled past finds themselves caught in a deadly conspiracy when a former colleague turns against them, embarking on a thrilling journey of redemption and revenge as they navigate a world of shadows and secrets.

A detective races against time to catch a serial killer who leaves behind a trail of cryptic symbols, leading to a hidden secret that holds the key to their identity.

In a claustrophobic submarine deep beneath the ocean, a crew must uncover the identity of a saboteur threatening to sink the vessel before it's too late.

In a city plagued by a string of unsolvable disappearances, a detective encounters a mysterious figure who seems to possess the ability to manipulate shadows and control the minds of others.

A renowned art forger is forced to help a detective solve a high-profile art theft, but as they get closer to the truth, they realize that not everything is as it seems.

A rookie police officer is assigned to a haunted precinct where the spirits of deceased criminals torment the living, forcing the officer to confront their own fears while solving a string of bizarre crimes.

A detective is assigned to protect a witness in a high-profile trial, but soon realizes that there is a mole within their own team, leading to a thrilling game of trust and betrayal.

In a city where no one can be trusted, a detective must navigate a labyrinth of lies and deceit to solve a murder that seems to have no motive, only to discover a shocking connection that turns the investigation upside down.

In a future where memories can be implanted and altered, a detective investigates a memory crime syndicate that erases and manipulates people's memories for their own nefarious purposes.

A detective investigates a series of mysterious disappearances in a small coastal town, only to discover a hidden underground society operating beneath the waves.

On a space station orbiting a distant planet, a detective must solve a murder that occurs during an experiment involving time dilation, where the flow of time becomes distorted.

An art thief is pulled into a treacherous heist involving stolen masterpieces, double-crossing associates, and a hidden agenda that threatens to expose their criminal past.

In a city populated by advanced AI-driven robots, a detective is assigned to investigate the first case of a robot developing emotions and committing a crime, leading to a thought-provoking exploration of artificial intelligence and morality.

A retired synchronized swimming champion finds herself caught up in a wave of intrigue and mystery when a precious underwater artifact disappears during an exhibition, prompting her to dive into the investigation and make a splash.

A journalist uncovers a string of unsolved disappearances in a small town and teams up with a detective to expose a dark secret hidden beneath the surface.

A brilliant engineer with a knack for technology becomes the prime suspect in a cybercrime investigation, leading them on a race against time to clear their name and uncover the true identity of the hacker responsible.

A renowned journalist with a nose for truth and a knack for investigation becomes immersed in a dangerous world of corruption and conspiracy, following the breadcrumbs of evidence to expose a far-reaching criminal network.

A reclusive botanist living in a secluded forest must uncover the truth behind a series of mysterious plant-related crimes that threaten the delicate balance of nature, revealing a hidden world of botanical secrets.

In a small coastal town, a detective investigates a murder that is intricately tied to the local fishing industry and a long-standing feud between rival families.

In the bustling world of professional sports, a retired athlete turned detective must investigate a match-fixing scandal that threatens to tarnish the integrity of the game, delving into the competitive world of athletes, agents, and illicit deals.

In a high-security prison, a prisoner-turned-detective works to prove their innocence in a murder case that occurred within the prison walls.

In a futuristic city where memories can be bought and sold, a detective investigates a black market operation that involves the illegal trade of stolen memories.

A mountain climber with a troubled past finds themselves in a perilous situation when a fellow climber goes missing during an expedition, embarking on a treacherous journey to unravel the mystery of the mountain's deadly secrets.

In a lawless frontier town, a tough gunslinger-turned-sheriff takes on a gang of outlaws terrorizing the locals, leading to a high-noon showdown that will determine the fate of the town.

In the picturesque world of winemaking, a sommelier with a refined palate must uncork the truth when a prized vintage disappears from a prestigious vineyard, uncorking a mystery that uncovers secrets hidden within the vine rows.

A detective is assigned to a case involving stolen artwork, but soon discovers that the paintings hold a deeper secret that could unravel the art world.

In a city where time moves backwards every other day, a detective investigates a murder that occurs during a time reversal, challenging the laws of cause and effect.

A charming bed and breakfast owner with a warm smile and a natural curiosity becomes an amateur sleuth when strange occurrences disrupt the peaceful atmosphere, prompting them to uncover the lighthearted truth behind the mysteries.

A detective finds themselves trapped in a cat-and-mouse game with a cunning serial killer who leaves behind cryptic clues in the form of intricate origami sculptures.

A graffiti artist with a message to convey finds themselves entangled in a dangerous game of cat and mouse with an art thief, using their artistic skills to tag their way to the truth.

In the gritty underworld of organized crime, a street-smart hustler with a troubled past must navigate a dangerous web of deceit and betrayal to protect their loved ones, leading to a thrilling game of cat and mouse with the crime syndicate.

The sleepy town of Meadowbrook is shaken when a mischievous gnome sculpture suddenly appears in the center of the town square, triggering a series of humorous yet perplexing crimes that leave the townsfolk scratching their heads.

In a city where everyone communicates through interpretive dance, a detective must unravel a murder case through the intricate language of movement.

A detective investigates a series of unexplained supernatural phenomena, leading them to question their own sanity and uncover a hidden world where the line between reality and the supernatural is blurred.

A talented pickpocket with a troubled upbringing becomes an accidental detective when they stumble upon a criminal plot that hits close to home, using their nimble fingers and street smarts to outsmart the dangerous underworld and protect their loved ones.

A professional gambler suspects foul play when an influential high-roller suddenly dies, initiating an investigation amidst the lavish surroundings.

A detective uncovers a secret society within law enforcement that is involved in organized crime, leading them to walk a dangerous tightrope between justice and corruption.

The tranquil world of birdwatching is disrupted when a rare species vanishes from the sanctuary, and an avid birdwatcher takes it upon themselves to follow the feathers and uncover the truth behind the avian mystery.

A talented safecracker is coerced into participating in a high-stakes heist orchestrated by a mysterious figure, pitting him against a ruthless crime lord and forcing him to confront his own past.

A theatrical director with a keen sense of observation and a flair for dramatics must uncover the truth when opening night at the community theater is marred by a mysterious disappearance, leading to a suspenseful investigation within the world of the stage.

A talented choreographer must unravel a web of envy and obsession when a rising star is found dead, using their understanding of movement and body language to uncover the truth.

An escape artist with an uncanny ability to break free from any situation becomes an accidental detective when they find themselves trapped in an elaborate heist, using their expertise in escapology to outsmart the cunning thieves.

A carnival performer with a knack for observation and showmanship becomes an accidental detective when a valuable carnival artifact disappears, thrusting them into a thrilling investigation full of carnival secrets.

In a society where advanced bioengineering is prevalent, a detective investigates a case involving the illegal cloning and black-market trade of human organs, leading to a dangerous conspiracy involving powerful corporations.

A fearless athlete with a hunger for adrenaline becomes an amateur sleuth when a fellow competitor is killed during a dangerous competition, racing against time to unmask the murderer before they strike again.

A detective must solve a murder that mirrors the plot of an unpublished manuscript, uncovering a web of secrets and betrayal within the world of publishing.

In a suburban neighborhood where houses can talk, a detective investigates a case involving a murdered house and a network of interconnected homes that hold the key to solving the crime.

A detective races against time to find a missing child, following a trail of clues that leads them deep into the city's criminal underbelly.

In a world where genetic engineering is the norm, a detective must navigate a city divided by genetically enhanced individuals and uncover the truth behind a string of genetically targeted murders.

A master of disguise with a mysterious past finds themselves caught in a web of espionage and betrayal when they are tasked with infiltrating a dangerous criminal organization, using their skills to bring down the criminal empire from within.

In a parallel universe where food is sentient, a detective is assigned to solve the murder of a famous vegetable celebrity, uncovering a conspiracy that threatens the delicate balance between humans and food.

A fashion designer with a flair for style and a talent for observation becomes an accidental detective when a priceless accessory disappears from a glamorous runway show, leading to a catwalk-worthy reveal.

In a stranded train stuck on a remote railway, a detective onboard must identify the killer among the passengers before the train is freed and the culprit escapes.

In a corrupt police department, a rogue detective battles against internal corruption while investigating a series of murders tied to a powerful crime family.

At a lively comedy club known for its hilarious acts, a stand-up comedian turned amateur investigator must crack the case of a stolen punchline, navigating through laughter and intrigue to unmask the joker responsible.

A detective is confronted with a series of unsolvable crimes that bear an eerie resemblance to a legendary detective's unsolved cases, prompting them to retrace the steps of their predecessor and unravel a mind-bending mystery.

A travel blogger with a curious spirit and a talent for uncovering hidden gems stumbles upon a series of light-hearted crimes during their adventures around the world, leading to unexpected discoveries and charming resolutions.

In a sleepy seaside town, a retired detective with a haunting past must confront a decades-old cold case that resurfaces, leading them on a suspenseful journey to uncover the truth and bring long-overdue justice to the victims.

In a small coastal village haunted by a tragic past, a paranormal investigator with a sixth sense must confront the supernatural when a series of ghostly apparitions lead them on a chilling journey to uncover the truth behind a long-kept secret.

An art restorer with a passion for historical artifacts becomes an accidental detective when they discover a hidden painting with a dark past, unraveling a centuries-old mystery and risking their own life in the pursuit of truth.

In a post-apocalyptic wasteland, a lone detective takes on a dangerous mission to retrieve stolen supplies that could save their community from starvation.

A master linguist with an ear for languages becomes an accidental detective when they uncover a cryptic message that leads them on a globe-trotting quest to stop an international conspiracy, deciphering codes and languages to prevent a catastrophic event.

A detective is assigned to protect a key witness in a dangerous gang trial, but soon realizes that the witness has secrets of their own that could upend the case.

A master thief with a code of honor is compelled to solve a murder in their tight-knit criminal underworld, seeking justice and protecting their own reputation.

In a town where all the residents spontaneously turn into animals at night, a detective investigates a crime committed during the peculiar transformation hour.

In a post-war setting, a detective must navigate the ruins of a city while investigating a series of crimes committed by individuals seeking revenge for wartime atrocities.

A passionate culinary critic turned amateur sleuth must solve a murder that occurs during a prestigious cooking competition, navigating a culinary landscape filled with rivalries, secrets, and delectable dishes.

In a gritty noir-inspired city, a hardboiled detective battles against corruption in the police force as they uncover a conspiracy that reaches the highest levels of power.

In a haunted hotel during a thunderstorm, a group of strangers must work together to solve a series of supernatural murders that mirror the hotel's dark history.

In a city ruled by corrupt politicians, a detective uncovers a web of conspiracy and power plays that reach far beyond the criminal underworld.

In the fast-paced world of journalism, an intrepid reporter with a nose for truth becomes immersed in a dangerous conspiracy that threatens to silence their investigation, fighting against powerful forces to expose the shocking secrets hidden in the shadows.

In a near-future society, a detective investigates a series of cybernetic augmentations gone wrong, uncovering a dark conspiracy that threatens the line between human and machine.

In a future where dreams can be accessed and manipulated, a detective delves into a series of crimes committed within the dream world, tracking down a criminal who can control nightmares.

A chocolatier finds themselves embroiled in a sweet yet puzzling mystery when their prized chocolate recipe is stolen, propelling them on a delectable investigation to unmask the chocolate thief.

In a foggy seaside town, a detective investigates a series of mysterious deaths that occur whenever the church bell tolls at midnight.

A wedding planner-turned-sleuth finds herself caught up in a whirlwind of intrigue and mystery when a bride-to-be disappears on the eve of her wedding, requiring the planner to uncover the truth behind the vanishing act.

A codebreaker with a talent for deciphering hidden messages must crack a complex cipher that holds the key to a long-forgotten secret, unveiling a web of intrigue and danger.

In a post-alien-invasion world, a detective joins forces with a former extraterrestrial collaborator to solve a murder that reveals a hidden alliance between humans and aliens.

A detective investigates a series of seemingly unrelated murders, only to realize that they are all connected by a common thread that hits close to home.

A talented magician with a flair for illusion must uncover the truth behind a series of baffling magic tricks that go awry, delving into the realm of deception and misdirection.

A detective is assigned to protect a key witness in a high-profile case, but as they dig deeper, they uncover a conspiracy that reaches the highest levels of government, endangering both their lives and the case itself.

A disgraced detective gets a chance at redemption when they are tasked with solving a high-profile murder that involves the city's elite and a tangled web of deceit.

A detective is called to investigate a series of mysterious deaths in a remote village, each victim found with an enigmatic symbol left behind, creating an air of foreboding.

In a world where genetic modification is commonplace, a detective investigates a series of murders targeting genetically enhanced individuals, unraveling a conspiracy that challenges the boundaries of human evolution.

In a dystopian city governed by a totalitarian regime, a resourceful rebel with a thirst for freedom becomes an accidental detective when they stumble upon a secret resistance movement, using their cunning and courage to expose the truth and ignite a revolution.

A competitive crossword puzzle solver embarks on a puzzling adventure beyond the newspaper grids when a fellow solver's sudden disappearance hints at a puzzle-filled treasure hunt with unexpected twists and turns.

A detective must solve a murder that takes place in a locked luxury penthouse, with a limited number of suspects who all seem to have unbreakable alibis.

A hard-boiled private eye is hired to track down a stolen artifact with immense value, encountering femme fatales, double-crossing criminals, and a conspiracy that goes deeper than anticipated.

A family moves into a seemingly perfect suburban neighborhood, only to discover that their neighbors are part of a cult that commits horrifying crimes, forcing them to fight for their lives and escape the neighborhood's grip.

In a small-town police station, a rookie cop and a seasoned detective team up to solve a complex homicide case that exposes deep-rooted corruption within the force.

A detective must navigate the dangerous world of underground fighting to solve a murder that occurred during an illegal tournament.

A young detective with extraordinary deduction skills is called upon to solve a locked-room mystery that has baffled investigators for years.

A detective with a troubled past is assigned to a case involving a serial killer who targets individuals connected to the detective's own dark secret.

An expert mixologist with a flair for creating unique cocktails finds themselves shaken, not stirred, when a rare and valuable spirit vanishes from their bar, launching them into a spirited investigation to recover the missing drink.

In a city plagued by supernatural occurrences, a detective with a skeptical mind is forced to confront the unexplainable as they investigate a series of paranormal crimes.

A forensic anthropologist with an uncanny ability to read bones becomes the key investigator in a series of mysterious murders, piecing together the skeletal remains to unveil the truth hidden beneath the surface.

In a dystopian society ruled by surveillance, a hacker with a rebellious spirit must uncover a government conspiracy and protect the freedom of the people, using their technological prowess to expose the truth and spark a revolution.

In a derelict underground tunnel system, a group of
urban explorers encounters a malevolent presence
that preys on their deepest fears, pushing them
to the brink of madness and survival.

A detective is assigned to protect a young witness who
possesses vital information about a powerful crime
syndicate, but the closer they get to the truth, the higher
the stakes become, leading to a heart-pounding climax.

In a vibrant carnival setting, a fearless carnival worker
with a knack for escapology finds themselves in a thrilling
race against time to rescue a kidnapped performer, using
their extraordinary skills to outwit the captors.

In a world where gravity fluctuates unpredictably, a
detective follows a trail of bizarre thefts committed by
a criminal who can control gravitational forces.

A talented illusionist with a troubled past becomes embroiled in a dangerous game of deception when their most daring trick is used to commit a crime, forcing them to use their skills to unveil the true identity of the mastermind behind the illusion.

A detective is pulled into a twisted game of cat and mouse with a cunning and elusive art thief, but as the investigation unfolds, they discover that there is more at stake than just stolen paintings.

A talented illusionist with a troubled past must confront their demons when a series of mysterious disappearances occurs within the magic community, uncovering a dark underworld where illusions become deadly.

A detective with a photographic memory and an uncanny ability to reconstruct crime scenes finds themselves entangled in a complex conspiracy involving high-profile individuals.

A writer's obsession with death and the macabre takes a dark turn when they find themselves entangled in a real-life conspiracy involving stolen corpses and secret medical experiments.

A group of retirees with a taste for adventure and a passion for solving puzzles form an amateur detective club, tackling light-hearted crimes that arise within their retirement community, proving that age is just a number when it comes to solving mysteries.

In a world where virtual reality is the ultimate escape, a detective is called to investigate a murder that takes place within a popular VR game, blurring the lines between reality and fantasy.

A puppet maker with a penchant for craftsmanship becomes an amateur detective when a rare and valuable puppet disappears, prompting them to pull the strings of intrigue and unravel the puppeteer behind the theft.

A detective infiltrates an underground cult that claims to have the ability to foresee crimes before they happen, but discovers a far more sinister truth behind their predictions.

A talented street artist with a keen eye for detail becomes an accidental detective when their graffiti art reveals a hidden message that leads them on a colorful chase through the city's vibrant streets.

A talented stage actor must step into the role of detective when a series of mysterious accidents threatens to sabotage the opening night, unmasking the true identity of the curtain's malevolent saboteur.

A disillusioned detective investigates a series of mysterious disappearances that are linked to an underground gambling ring, revealing a web of corruption, greed, and dangerous alliances.

A detective is assigned to a case involving a mysterious
art forger whose work threatens to disrupt the
art world and unveil long-held secrets.

A gifted profiler with a deep understanding of the criminal
mind finds themselves in a race against time to stop a serial
killer who leaves behind intricate puzzles and clues, unlocking
the twisted psyche of the killer before they strike again.

A detective must confront their own past when a serial
killer resurfaces after years of silence, forcing them to
relive the traumatic events that nearly destroyed them.

A detective is assigned to protect a key witness in a high-profile
trial, but they soon realize that there is a leak within their own
department, forcing them to question who they can trust.

In a picturesque village known for its wine making traditions, a knowledgeable sommelier must uncork the truth behind a poisoned vintage, tracing the grapes back to their vineyard origins to unmask the culprit and save the reputation of the wine industry.

In a remote lighthouse on a stormy night, a lighthouse keeper discovers a body washed ashore, sparking an investigation that uncovers dark secrets hidden within the isolated structure.

In a city where human consciousness can be transferred into artificial bodies, a detective discovers a string of murders targeting those who have undergone the process, uncovering a conspiracy that questions the nature of identity and existence.

A disgraced former detective is given a chance at redemption when a wealthy socialite hires him to find her missing husband, thrusting him into a deadly game of deception and betrayal.

A seasoned detective becomes embroiled in a dangerous game of power and corruption within the police force, uncovering a network of dirty cops and unraveling the truth behind a high-profile case.

A determined Pinkerton detective is hired to solve a mysterious train robbery, unraveling a plot that involves a notorious gang of bandits and a hidden cache of stolen gold.

In a world where memory manipulation is possible, a detective uncovers a conspiracy involving the alteration of memories for personal gain.

In a bustling hospital emergency room, a doctor begins to suspect foul play when a series of patients with similar symptoms unexpectedly die, launching a secret investigation within the hospital.

A gifted film editor with a keen eye for detail must unravel a conspiracy that threatens to destroy a renowned director's reputation, piecing together the clues hidden within the footage to reveal the truth.

In a lawless border town, a brave and resourceful marshal must bring down a ruthless gang of rustlers who are stealing cattle and terrorizing the local ranchers.

A talented linguist with a talent for deciphering ancient languages becomes embroiled in a race against time when an ancient artifact is stolen, using their linguistic expertise to unravel an ancient prophecy and prevent a catastrophic event.

A small town is gripped by fear as a serial killer known as "The Midnight Phantom" strikes every night, leaving behind cryptic clues inspired by ancient folklore.

On a colonized planet inhabited by alien species, a detective from Earth investigates a murder that unveils tensions between different alien races and challenges the fragile peace.

In the world of high-end fashion, a talented fashion photographer becomes embroiled in a murder investigation that uncovers a dark underworld of exploitation, drugs, and twisted desires.

A detective must solve a murder in a secluded village where everyone has a hidden motive, unraveling a complex web of lies and deceit.

In an opulent art gallery after hours, a renowned art thief must navigate a maze of laser security systems and rival criminals to steal a priceless masterpiece.

A sharpshooter-turned-detective is hired to solve the murder of a prominent landowner, facing resistance from the corrupt local law enforcement and unmasking a web of secrets and lies.

A culinary aficionado with a discerning palate must solve a tantalizing mystery involving stolen recipes and cutthroat competition, dishing up a thrilling investigation spiced with unexpected twists.

In a world where advanced genetic engineering is used to create designer pets, a detective unravels a case involving the illegal modification and smuggling of genetically enhanced animals, revealing a dark underworld.

A detective races against time to track down a serial killer who leaves behind intricate puzzles, leading to a heart-stopping revelation that the killer might be closer than anyone could have imagined.

In a dystopian future, a detective must solve a murder that challenges the oppressive regime, risking their own life in the process.

In a forgotten asylum on the outskirts of town, a detective investigates a series of gruesome murders that seem to be connected to the dark history of the institution and the vengeful spirits within.

In a post-apocalyptic world, a resourceful scavenger with a troubled past must uncover the truth behind a series of mysterious disappearances in their settlement, leading them on a perilous journey through the desolate wasteland.

A detective must solve a murder that seems to be connected to a long-lost treasure map, leading them on a perilous journey filled with treacherous obstacles and hidden dangers.

A cursed artifact surfaces, causing anyone who possesses it to succumb to madness and commit heinous crimes, leading a detective on a race against time to break the curse before they too fall victim.

In a small town plagued by supernatural occurrences, a detective with a skeptical mind must unravel the truth behind a series of inexplicable crimes.

In the competitive world of professional dance, a gifted dancer with a troubled past must unravel a tangled web of jealousy and obsession when a fellow dancer is brutally attacked, using their extraordinary talent and grace to expose the truth.

In a post-apocalyptic world, a detective roams the desolate streets, pursuing a deranged killer who stages elaborate crime scenes to maintain a twisted sense of normalcy in an unraveled society.

In a post-apocalyptic world, a resourceful survivor with a troubled past must navigate a dangerous wasteland to uncover the truth behind a series of mysterious disappearances, discovering that the greatest threat may come from within their own community.

A drifter with a haunted past becomes an accidental detective when a valuable gold shipment goes missing, thrusting them into a treacherous journey through rugged landscapes and dangerous encounters.

A detective, haunted by the loss of a loved one, must confront their own past when they are assigned to a case that eerily resembles a cold case they failed to solve.

A detective with synesthesia discovers that their unique ability to see colors and emotions can help them solve a series of murders with an otherworldly twist.

In a charming seaside town known for its fishing heritage, a resourceful fisherman turned amateur sleuth must solve the mystery behind a series of disappearances at sea, delving into the murky depths to uncover a haunting truth.

A fashion model turned amateur detective must solve the mystery behind a series of fashion sabotages that threaten to derail the biggest runway show of the year, revealing a cutthroat industry filled with secrets and rivalries.

A renowned art collector hosts a grand exhibition of rare and cursed artifacts, and a detective must unravel the enigmatic connection between the items and a series of inexplicable crimes.

A detective must solve a series of murders linked to a secret society that stages elaborate theatrical performances based on dark tales, with each act leading to a deadly finale.

A mysterious woman hires a cynical detective to find her missing sister, plunging him into a twisted plot involving a sadistic serial killer, dark secrets, and a race against time.

In a post-apocalyptic world, a detective uncovers a secret society that uses forbidden technology to alter memories, leading them on a dangerous journey to restore the truth.

A tightrope walker with a unique perspective and a sharp intuition becomes an amateur sleuth when a fellow performer vanishes under mysterious circumstances, revealing a dark underbelly behind the enchanting facade of the carnival.

In a small town filled with secrets, a detective investigates a murder that leads them to a hidden cult with sinister rituals, putting their own life on the line to uncover the truth.

In a suburban neighborhood where lawns come to life, a detective investigates a series of lawn gnome disappearances that reveal a hidden underground society of sentient garden ornaments.

In a tranquil village nestled in the countryside, a retired detective must confront a cold case from their past that resurfaces, forcing them to revisit old wounds and solve a mystery that has haunted them for years.

A martial artist with a tragic past becomes an accidental vigilante when they witness a brutal crime, using their exceptional combat skills to mete out justice and uncover the dark underbelly of the city's criminal underworld.

In a city governed by advanced holographic technology, a detective investigates a series of crimes committed by a holographic entity that can manifest in the physical world, blurring the line between reality and illusion.

A detective must navigate the cutthroat world of high-stakes gambling to solve a murder that occurred during an underground poker tournament.

An amnesiac detective wakes up with blood on their hands and a dead body nearby, embarking on a personal quest to unravel their own past while being pursued by both the law and ruthless criminals.

A parkour athlete with a troubled past becomes an accidental detective when a parkour competition turns deadly, leading them on a breathtaking chase across the cityscape to expose a hidden conspiracy.

A detective is called to a secluded mansion where a wealthy family's gathering takes a deadly turn, and they must unravel a web of lies, betrayals, and family secrets to find the killer.

A detective with cybernetic enhancements investigates a murder in a virtual reality game, where the line between the digital and physical worlds blurs.

A talented painter with a troubled conscience must navigate a dangerous underworld to expose a master forger and protect the integrity of the art world, blurring the lines between authenticity and deception.

In a charming bookstore known for its rare book collection, a bookworm with a thirst for knowledge must uncover the truth behind a mysterious ancient manuscript that holds the secrets to a forgotten civilization.

A detective investigates a series of crimes in a small town where superstitions and folklore play a significant role, discovering a dark history that links to the present.

In a bustling courtroom during a high-profile trial, a defense attorney must prove their client's innocence amidst a web of lies, corruption, and manipulation.

A notorious mob boss hires a street-smart private eye to recover a stolen ledger that holds the secrets of the criminal underworld, leading to a cat-and-mouse game of deception and danger.

In a bustling airport terminal, a detective races against time to prevent a terrorist attack orchestrated by a mysterious figure hiding among the crowd of travelers.

A fearless animal trainer with a deep connection to creatures of all kinds finds themselves embroiled in a mystery when a prized show animal is kidnapped, launching them on a wild chase to rescue the beloved creature.

A quirky amateur sleuth with a passion for crossword puzzles and a day job as a pet detective uncovers a series of animal-related crimes in their neighborhood, leading to a heartwarming resolution.

A forensic psychologist with a deep understanding of the human mind becomes an accidental detective when a series of bizarre crimes defy conventional explanations, delving into the twisted psyches of the perpetrators to uncover the chilling truth behind their motives.

In the world of underground pornography, a determined investigator exposes a ring of exploitation and abuse, seeking justice for the victims while risking their own safety.

A detective is called to a prestigious boarding school where a student has gone missing, but as they dig deeper, they discover a web of secrets involving the school's dark past.

In a small town plagued by unsolved mysteries, a curious librarian with a passion for books becomes an accidental detective when a rare manuscript goes missing, uncovering a trail of clues hidden within the pages of classic literature.

In a world where memory implants are a common practice, a detective investigates a series of mind-hacking crimes, where criminals manipulate and erase memories for their nefarious purposes.

A gifted mathematician with a love for puzzles becomes an accidental detective when a series of seemingly unrelated crimes are connected by a complex mathematical pattern, following the numbers to reveal the mastermind behind the calculated chaos.

As the carnival rolls into town, a former tightrope walker turned amateur detective must unravel the secrets hidden beneath the colorful tents when a valuable prize goes missing, resulting in a thrilling investigation full of carnival magic and unexpected twists.

A talented archaeologist with a knack for discovering ancient artifacts becomes an accidental detective when a priceless relic is stolen, leading them on a thrilling adventure through history to recover the artifact and uncover a hidden treasure.

A detective races against time to rescue a kidnapped child, but the closer they get to the truth, the more they realize that the real villain might not be who they initially suspected, leading to a suspenseful twist that changes everything.

A detective is drawn into the seedy underbelly of a city's criminal underworld as they pursue a notorious mastermind who employs a network of deceit and manipulation.

In a remote mountain village shrouded in legends, a folklore expert turned amateur detective must unravel the truth behind a series of eerie supernatural occurrences, delving into the realm of myth and superstition.

A brilliant mathematician with a knack for patterns and algorithms becomes an accidental detective when a seemingly unsolvable equation leads them to a hidden conspiracy that stretches the limits of logic.

In a city ruled by a powerful crime lord, a detective must navigate the dangerous underworld and outsmart the kingpin to bring justice to the streets.

A renowned psychologist finds themselves entangled in the twisted minds of serial killers, delving into the dark recesses of humanity to solve a series of chilling and sadistic crimes.

A talented cryptographer with a knack for cracking codes becomes embroiled in a thrilling conspiracy when they stumble upon a cryptic message that reveals a hidden plot, using their skills to decrypt the secrets and expose the mastermind.

A dog walker with a pack of loyal companions and a sharp eye for details finds themselves in the middle of a light-hearted canine caper, leading to a tail-wagging resolution that celebrates the bond between humans and their furry friends.

A locksmith with an affinity for puzzles finds themselves at the center of a heist when their unique locks are targeted by a group of master thieves, using their expertise to outwit the criminals and protect the secrets hidden behind the doors.

A sommelier with a refined palate becomes an accidental detective when a rare vintage is poisoned, uncorking a mystery that swirls with intrigue, jealousy, and the bitter taste of revenge.

In the atmospheric streets of a noir-inspired city, a hard-boiled detective with a cynical outlook must uncover a web of corruption that stretches from the police force to the highest levels of government, navigating treacherous alleys and shadowy figures to bring justice to the dark underbelly of the city.

A detective must solve a murder case that has eerie similarities to an unsolved mystery from their past, delving into the dark recesses of their own memories to uncover the truth.

In a near-future where climate change has ravaged the world, a detective investigates a murder that is somehow connected to a mysterious weather-manipulation technology.

In a picturesque vineyard known for its exquisite wines, a sommelier with an extraordinary palate becomes entangled in a wine-related mystery involving a rare vintage and a deadly secret hidden within the vineyards.

A cunning con artist poses as a renowned gunslinger to infiltrate a gang of thieves planning a major heist, leading to a thrilling game of deception and double-crossing.

A sharp-witted journalist with a nose for news becomes entangled in a dangerous conspiracy when they uncover a cover-up that threatens to shake the foundations of society, risking everything to expose the truth and protect the innocent.

In the picturesque world of horse racing, a seasoned jockey with a keen intuition becomes entangled in a race-fixing scandal, using their insider knowledge and racing instincts to expose the truth and restore integrity to the sport.

A detective is haunted by a case from their past, revisiting an unsolved murder that resurfaces in the present, forcing them to confront their own failures and seek redemption.

In the fast-paced world of professional racing, a talented race car driver with a need for speed must solve a mysterious crash that threatens to derail their career, uncovering a high-stakes conspiracy that goes beyond the finish line.

A detective must solve a murder that appears to be the work of a notorious serial killer who was believed to be dead for years.

A socialite with a flair for intrigue must solve a murder that occurs during a lavish gala, navigating a web of deceit and hidden motives that surround the elite.

In a city where crime is policed by drones and automated law enforcement systems, a detective investigates a glitch in the system that allows criminals to exploit its weaknesses and commit undetectable crimes.

A talented origami artist with a passion for paper folding finds themselves embroiled in a mysterious origami-themed crime spree, where each folded creation holds a clue to the next, leading to a captivating origami chase.

In a society where mind uploading is possible, a detective investigates a murder that takes place within a virtual world inhabited by uploaded consciousness, raising questions about identity and the nature of reality.

A detective must solve a murder that occurs in a grand theater during a highly anticipated opening night performance, with the entire cast and crew as potential suspects.

In a carnival-themed town where clowns are the ruling class, a detective tries to solve a murder at a circus where everyone is a potential suspect, including the victim who refuses to stay dead.

A jaded private investigator must navigate a web of celebrity secrets and scandals when a prominent actor goes missing, uncovering the dark underbelly of fame and fortune.

In a high-tech future where memories can be altered,
a detective investigates a series of crimes involving
memory manipulation, uncovering a conspiracy
that reaches the highest levels of society.

The captivating world of ballroom dancing becomes the
backdrop for a light-hearted mystery as a dance instructor must
uncover the truth behind a series of sabotaged performances,
waltzing their way through clues to find the culprits.

In a society divided by genetic purity, a detective investigates
a series of murders targeting individuals deemed genetically
impure, uncovering a sinister eugenics plot.

In a world where time loops are a common
occurrence, a detective finds themselves trapped
in a never-ending investigation where the crime
keeps repeating itself with slight variations.

In a small frontier community, a no-nonsense schoolmarm unravels a series of crimes committed by a secret gang of outlaws, leading to a clash between justice and lawlessness.

A detective must solve a murder in a futuristic city where advanced technology and virtual reality blur the lines between reality and illusion.

A detective with a troubled past is haunted by a cold case that resurfaces, leading them on a relentless pursuit of the truth and closure.

In a remote mountain village plagued by a decades-old curse, a brave detective with a connection to the supernatural must uncover the truth behind a series of mysterious deaths, confronting ancient folklore and malevolent forces that threaten to consume the entire community.

A journalist becomes the target of a serial killer after uncovering a dark secret that implicates powerful individuals in a series of heinous crimes.

In a small town where everyone knows everyone, a detective discovers that a long-standing cold case is connected to a series of recent murders, unraveling secrets that have been buried for decades.

A detective with a unique ability to see glimpses of the past must unravel a cold case that has remained unsolved for decades, following a trail of hidden clues.

A master puzzle maker is thrust into a real-life puzzle adventure when their intricate puzzle box becomes the center of a lighthearted mystery, challenging them to solve a series of mind-bending enigmas to unlock the truth.

A detective must solve a series of murders inspired by famous works of literature, piecing together the twisted mind of a killer who believes they are reenacting literary masterpieces.

On a distant planet colonized by humans, a detective uncovers a conspiracy involving a secret experiment that grants extraordinary powers to a select few, leading to a thrilling chase across the alien landscape.

A master chef with a refined palate and a talent for deduction finds themselves in a culinary mystery when a renowned food critic is poisoned during a high-profile dining event, leading the chef on a quest to unmask the killer hidden among the flavors.

A renowned archaeologist with a knack for unraveling ancient mysteries becomes embroiled in a race against time to recover a legendary artifact before it falls into the wrong hands, delving into forgotten civilizations and deciphering cryptic clues along the way.

An investigative journalist receives an anonymous tip about a corrupt politician, plunging them into a dangerous investigation that puts their life at risk.

A locksmith with a troubled past must confront their demons when a series of mysterious break-ins occur, leading them on a dangerous journey to uncover the truth behind the crimes and find redemption.

A detective is drawn into a dangerous world of underground street racing, where a series of accidents turn out to be deliberate acts of sabotage and revenge.

In a world where time travel is a reality, a detective is tasked with solving a paradoxical murder case that involves time loops, multiple versions of the same person, and altering timelines.

A criminal profiler with a deep understanding of the human psyche must unravel the twisted motives of a serial killer who leaves behind intricate psychological puzzles, using their expertise to anticipate the killer's next move and bring them to justice.